Woman on the Move

Woman on the Move
Unapologetic Poetry

Jasira Monique

© 2012 by Jasira Monique.

All rights reserved. No part of this book may be reproduced, stored in a retrieval system or transmitted in any form or by any means without the prior written permission of the publishers, except by a reviewer who may quote brief passages in a review to be printed in a newspaper, magazine or journal.

First printing

Cover Art Illustration by Jason Fleurant
http://www.fineartamerica.com/profiles/jason-fleurant.html

Front & Back Cover Design by iMedia Marketing Group, LLC
http://www.imediamarketinggrp.com

Back Cover Photography by HS Photography
http://www.hsphototime.com

ISBN: 0-61550-564-3
PUBLISHED BY BRUISED KISSES PUBLISHING, LLC

Printed in the United States of America

Reviews for *Woman on the Move* by Jasira Monique

'Jasira Monique's poems are honest and full of genuine emotion. She captures the essence of the struggle to not only know oneself, but also to show the world that truth as well. In "Every Person," she expresses our universal desire to be valued and loved, and in 'Everybody Can be Great," she emphasizes the contributions each individual can make to the world. Later in the collection, "Running on E" explores the perils of unrequited love and compassion, and the final poem in the collection "Starlight Encryption," is a heartfelt ode to a lover. Overall, this is an inspirational collection that is both uplifting and sincere'
Africa Fine, Professor & Author of Swan

'A book of poetry that speaks to the modern woman in her native tongue, giving rise to her inner urban Amazon'
Safiya Songhai, Student Emmy Award-winning American film director

'*Women on the Move* takes readers on a journey into different stages of discovery in a women's life. Jasira Monique's heart is expressed through her poetry, her words are captivating and with each poem readers are engulfed into a new experience. I believe elements of romance, self-love and empowerment flow through the pages of this book'
Vicky S. Joseph, Actor & Spoken Word Poet

'I was thoroughly impressed. This is the type of poetry that speaks to its reader: personal and inspirational. It has an unmistakable modern-day flow that weaves smoothly in and out of stories'
TaRhonda Thomas ~ KUSA-TV (Denver, CO)

'Woman on the Move takes the reader on a beautiful, lyrical journey through the emotions that we all feel. With a variety of poems on the issues of life, this book has something we all can feel. Kudos to Monique for sharing her joy and pain in such a generous way!'
A'ndrea J. Wilson, Author of Wife 101

'Woman on the move is a great compilation of the artist's thoughts, neatly compacted into a thought provoking and poetic flow. If you are a lover of poetry and spoken word, surely you will appreciate Jasira Monique's heart infused collection'
Kimberly Matthews-Hooker, Author of The Perfect Shoe

'Jasira Monique delivers hard truths to her readers about the struggles of a woman solidifying her legacy. Love will change; growth is a necessary pain, the imperfect balance of family and self, delivered in writing so consoling in its honesty that you completely embrace the notion of success being the only option'
Angelina Nicole, Poet

DEDICATION

This collection of poetry is dedicated to every moment whether encouraging or the opposite that made me appreciate life and the power to love more. I salute the healing power of poetry and what it does for us. I thank every person that ignited a spark of creativity in me that helped me use words to embellish paper. This book is dedicated to all who have conquered their fears, naysayers and embraced the good within themselves when their light was diminishing. I salute you for pulling through and choosing the will to live and to love. This book is dedicated to those who fight every day to win the battle of the mind.

CONTENTS

Chapter I: Gravity Can't Hold Me Down

My Equilibrium Is Off — 1

gifted.i.am — 4

Fantastic — 6

Spaceship Status — 8

Naked Ambition — 10

Woman On The Move — 12

Chapter II: Elevated Thoughts

John Coltrane's Equinox — 15

Caution's End — 16

Every Person — 17

Healthy Thinkers — 18

Magical Music — 20

Everybody Can Be Great — 21

Chapter III: A Woman's Work Never Ends

My Tick Tock 25

May I 26

The Astrologist 27

Give Me a Spanish Moss Tree at Noon 28

Tell Your Purse to Move! 30

Love I Do 32

Chapter IV: The Truth Hurts

Livin' Just Wasn't Worth It 35

A Fallen Black Queen's Contradictions 37

The Land of Better Yet 38

Running on E 41

Woman On the Move's Dilemma 42

Awakened 44

Chapter V: Taking No Prisoners

Counter-Clockwise — 47

Bold As You Like It — 48

Big Talk, Little Feet — 49

Temporary Resolve — 50

Blacknogstic — 53

Why Aren't You Proud To Be Black? — 55

Support or Abort — 57

Pause — 58

America's New Bandit — 60

Chapter VI: Sacrificial Love

My Little Champion — 69

Chocolate Moon — 70

My Garden's Empty — 71

Seashell Whispers — 73

With Love & At Peace — 74

Sascha Skylar — 76

Starlight Encryption — 77

FOREWORD

I stepped in the door of a Progressive Women's Business Network Luncheon and was greeted by a woman whose light was so bright, whose spirit was so warm and loving, and whose personality was infectious. Yes...it was Jasira Monique. Until that point, we hadn't met in person. We had a virtual relationship via Twitter and Facebook. When she said, "@SocialMediaVIP!!!" I was caught off guard in a very pleasant way. But who could deny that friendly smile and greeting? From that moment, I have had the pleasure of watching a powerful and amazing woman's journey unfold in a way that has left me speechless.

Ironically, this book of poetry is a "glimpse into the lives of undeniably bold, charismatic and unstoppable women." Its author is one of those women. It is said that courage is not the absence of fear, but the acknowledgment of something greater. Jasira Monique is a symbol of courage. She has embraced her gifts, talents and blessings and used them to touch the lives of others. While paying it forward, she uses them to create opportunities she initially thought were unattainable. She has stepped outside her comfort zone and stretched herself to new heights. Not the least bit self-absorbed, she is constantly sharing resources and encouraging others to be their best.

As I read through this beautiful book of poetry, I was entertained, edified, and inspired. I was reminded that although we will encounter challenges throughout our lifetime, this book is the product of enduring those challenges and turning them all into something magnificent. Jasira Monique's light, spirit and personality shine through in every verse.

Allow this book to help you tap into those forgotten dreams, push past those doubts or simply take your life to the next level. Become unstoppable!

Suzzette Turnbull
CEO, Social Media for Entertainers

Chapter 1:
Gravity Can't Hold Me Down

"I'm so bright that my words make light of the stars"

— *gifted.i.am*

MY EQUILIBRIUM IS OFF

Catastrophic events have taken place
My love has deviated to the Earth's core
My mind is inebriated
With thoughts that can run the
Pacific Ocean dry

Sweet, voluptuous & sexy
But I'm hellacious as they get
Don't test me!
My equilibrium is off
I want balance
I want my love rocked back
To its origin

I want initiation
Initiation that foreign luxury cars have
From virgin drivers who
Thirst for adventure
Shifting gears into tunnels
That lead to moonlit skies
In France
At 120 miles per hour
I want excitement
Like every time you see me
Like every moment
With me is Christmas

I want soft wet kisses

I want pretty pink toes

Painted by you

And back rubs

And a love so strong

So deep

That it balances my body

In a way that makes

All the gravity that sustains us

Seem inexistent

I want you

I want you more than I want cute shoes and diamonds

And more than I want a 'like' clicked on Facebook

By my favorite emcee

I want my existence in your life

To be more appreciated

Than 608 revolving texts from the sexiest women on Earth

Who'll never know you or love you like I do

My equilibrium is off

And I need balance

I've got the best love coming at me

Like a Earthquake at 8.9

How can I ignore

A love like yours

You made it absolutely impossible

For me to ignore you

I tried

I hope you remember

Now your love has saturated

Every item I own, piece of clothing & even my skin

Smells like you

I sometimes find myself

Using your gestures

Yes, my equilibrium is off

It's so off I'm not sure I know what I want

You've somehow evolved in my space

So much to where it feels like yours

Your clothes

Your clothes are hanging in my closet

And the only thing I think

Is does he mind if I

Wear this

I find myself feeling awkward around other men

Like other men are literally Mars

and I'm Venus

I don't even look at other men

The same way I used to

The day before I met you

My equilibrium is... waiting

gifted.i.am

He said I was gifted

I said 'You're right'

I got blessings

Like monumental gifts

That wake me up by sunlight

I got melodies so heavenly

They stay melodious

In my sleep

My thoughts are deep

But my mind is never low

I got gifts to behold

Like words never told

But saved for the present

So I hope he likes presents

Because I'm gifted

I'm so lifted

That I write up high

Like innovations can fly

I'm so bright

That my words make light of the stars

My mind is never far

From him

I channel our past

So he can turn to our future

And make light of it

Like I don't remember when...

He didn't love me

Because ever since I

Entered his life

And he in mine

I realized that

I was gifted

Like ironically

The Earth tilted

And the Moon met the Sun

Mathematically we stood

In a place of Time & Space

Bold & Courageous African love

That our ancestors conjured up

And I never knew a

Better way to love

Than to give gifts from up above

And delight in balance

Like my equilibrium

Is still seeking balance

But gifted.i.am

FANTASTIC

They said I'll never make it
So I had to shut 'em down &
Take it
Top notch
So hot
I'm bakin'

Back & forth
Like Aaliyah
Diamond studded like Trina
Shine so bright
You need a light?
Im yo heala

I got poetry on lock
Like on Tamarind
Them goons got glocks
Harder in the paint
Than Wocka Flock

Let me elevate you
Celebrate you
They want to break you
But let me make you
My Bruised Kisses pupil

Thank you

For listenin'

To everything yo soul

Has been whisperin'

Jasira Monique is not a rapper

Rather

A master of all words that gather

So hot with pen & paper

Or even on my droid

You can call me Poetry's Master

SPACESHIP STATUS

(Dedicated to a phenomenal Denver poet, Jai Harris)

See when I tell you
Rockets couldn't blast
My flow
There's no limit to how far
I'll go
I expected you to believe me

You don't have to be beneath me
Although I'm like a mountain
I expect you to reach me
Or die tryin'
Aint no sense in lyin'
This high is fantastic

Not that you can catch it
See my elevation
Took your revelation
Somewhere to crash it
I told you this high is that habit

Once you have it
The clouds can't grasp it
MLK, JFK and MJJ
Had dreams of nations that moonwalked

But they couldn't pass it

See I lit the torch
And I expect you to pass it
Once you grasp it
It's up to you
To let the next man catch it
Mold them, elevate 'em,
Then let him live to surpass it
Spaceship status.

NAKED AMBITION

People who are confident
With themselves
While by themselves
Are confident
Around others

Solitary confinement
Is prison to some
But who are you
In a room by yourself
With locked doors?

Does the smell of your prayers reach the heavens
Does the prickles in your knees remind you
Of the power of oneness with God
With your temple to the ground
And your toes curled tight

Delve deep into your
Memories of love lost, life restored and hope reknewed
Expose fears of failure, time running out and loneliness
And relinquish the power
That held you from
Loving you
When you, needed you the most

Being your best friend
Should be your daily ambition
Being good to yourself
Shows others
How to treat you

Accept all of your flaws
And imperfections as such
God loves you as you should love yourself
Unconditionally
When in God's love alone
You unconsciously
Allow others to accept you
In all of your nakedness
Pure and at peace

WOMAN ON THE MOVE

I came

and I left

As quick as a last breath

How can a thief of hearts be heartless?

I desire to achieve my dreams

By any means

So don't fault me

For being faultless

Love?

Love is everlasting

My life forever passin'

I desire freedom

Freedom to not regret

Loving too much

See I'd rather love too little than too much

Because love once depleted

Diminishes the soul

How can a poet

Delve into literary realms of love

If the poet never stepped away to write

My thirst for literature that uplifts and ignites

Won't allow me to lie

Complacently in love at night

My mind desires elevation

With other minds

who seek to challenge mass communication

Emptiness of thoughts and social repetitiveness

Are not my flavors of morning brew

Together there's not too much

We can't do

But I have to warn you

I'm a woman

on the move

Chapter 99: Elevated Thoughts

"I await a drum major that will lead the steps to redemption"

– Magical Music

JOHN COLTRANE'S EQUINOX

I'm a fan of all that is marvelous
Anything relevant
To the unimaginable
Quest
Your love can provide

I am partner to all that is peaceful
Anything consistent
To the unpredictable
Journey
Your friendship can form

I am a lover of all that is pure
Anything innocent
To the tornado like
Odyssey
That awaits those who are living

I am a master of all that is uncertain
Anything ambiguous
To the brilliant
Path of those who seek wisdom

CAUTION'S END

Many people marvel at the what if's
The overused colloquialism
"It's not as easy as it looks"
What about letting
Go of what's simple what's easy
Unlock the difficult
Release the hard &
Open the door
Rebuild your confidence
By remembering
All the previous closed doors
All the no's
All of the "how do you plan to do that?"
And remember who brought you
To your initial success
Believe that your life
Has an amazing purpose &
You have a magnificent
Role in life's future
Live life with passion & conviction
You owe it to you
To be your best
& live without regret
Time is the only thing that
Will certainly never come back

EVERY PERSON

Every person

Every man

Every woman

Wants to feel there Is

Something so intrinsically different

About their existence

From the next

Everyone desires

That unique appeal

That infinitely massive

Benefit of knowing

We are valued

Greater than

Any other person

On the face of this Earth

By the one we love

Or the one

That Love chose to lend us

Every woman

Every man

Every person

Deserves that love

HEALTHY THINKERS

Power & purpose
When combined with
Passion & conviction
Have astonishing results

Thoughts paint pictures
Of your future
Memories display moments
Of your past

Rework your mind's appetite
Discipline it
To become a master
At living your dreams
Not your fears

Ever wonder what inspired
The creation of
Pyramids or castles?

The human capacity for thinking &
Realizing our thoughts
Into actions
By discipline & determination
Is worth discussion

Promote healthy thought patterns
By surrounding yourself
With healthy thinkers
Think amazing thoughts
Reinforce in your mind's appetite
How marvelous you are to the Earth

How gifted is your presence
To those who surround you
When hurt and disappointed
Remember that life is
Seeking balance in your love
Love will balance your
Thoughts and life

Your thoughts create powerful
Moments, memories and
Bring you to exactly where
You need to be
Always remember the power
Of healthy thoughts and words
Someone spoke you into being &
Their actions brought you here…..

MAGICAL MUSIC

My eyes gaze slowly at the curtain

I await the songstress

To sing a song of love

Beauty

Triumph

Passion

And to leave me with an insatiable desire

To sing her song forever

I await a moment in music

That will transcend all time

A moment of defeat

Hurt

Anger

Rage

And challenge me to

Exorcise the demons of mediocrity

And self-doubt

Let's enter the stanza playing freedom

Peace

Hope

And with his rim shot

Ignite the passion in all of us

that comes from knowing

That this music can live in our minds forever

Yes, forever

Magical Music...

EVERYBODY CAN BE GREAT

(Dedicated to Dr. Martin Luther King Jr.)

'Everybody can be great
because everybody can serve'
everybody can love
everybody can give

Everybody has the ability
to smile
to laugh
to hug
to cheer

Everybody has the ability
to touch a hand
to hold a hand
to grab a hand
and to steer someone else from doing wrong

Everybody has the propensity
to know when a friend is in need
to know when a child is lost
to know when a debt isn't paid
to know when someone needs shelter

Everybody has the ability
to stand for what is right

to speak up for those who are wronged

to knock down a barrier someone else put up

to open a door someone else closed

You have a right

to know you are loved

to know you are important

to know you are great

to know that God considers you worthy

We have a right

to love others

to feed the hungry

to clothe the poor

to protest injustice

to serve our brothers and sisters of all races and nationalities

to not support the mistreatment of others

Everybody can be great because everybody can serve

and show others who God is through their service done in humility.

23 | Woman on the Move

Chapter III: A Woman's Work Never Ends

"Never settle your bag in one place for too long. Tell your purse to move and it will lead you to where it belongs"

– **Tell Your Purse to Move**

THE TICK TOCK

My mind keeps time of footsteps

Each click clack

Symbolizes the tick tock

Of my mind's mental clock

Every tick tock is anotha' second

Closer to anotha' dolla'

So I neva' botha'

Wastin' time

Wastin' time

Is like wasting rhymes

My time is precious

And my words are never cheap

Neither can I eva' afford to waste

So I neva' slow the pace

I just work

Get it done

No time for idle ways, sudden delays or foolery

My mind keeps time of footsteps

No betta' help is she

Who makes her own pay

And creates her own way

Of makin' it

Neva fakin' it

But gettin' it done

Cuz as long as that clock is tickin'

My dollars I'm gettin' on this clock!

MAY I

May I read you a book

To open up your mind

To endless dreams

Can I open the door

So you can enter

A world of abundant streams

Should I cook you dinner

To satisfy your

Belly's desire to be filled with creativity

Will I run you a bath

So you can purify

Your mind from all

Of the world's extremities

Do I sit here and wait

To rub your back

As you lay patiently

Waiting to release

All of today's worries

Learn to release & recycle 'green energy'

May I read you a book

To open up your mind

To endless dreams

May I open the door

And take you with me

THE ASTROLOGIST

Her mind opened me up

To sights unseen

She took me back home

Summoned the Universe

And gave birth to

Jasira Queen

Her mouth beckoned the handsome sun

He formed symbols through children's books

To increase my propensity

To tell a story

So vividly as I should

Her diligence led me to discover

That love is only as loving

As you make it

And can be so powerful

When it's unconditional

I craved her presence and wisdom

Because she dug deep into the craters of my surface

And saw the depth of me

That was once hidden

Beyond the galaxy

Banished from the sky's radiance

Her love and premonition

Made my light shine and gave me

Freedom to live at home amongst the planets

GIVE ME A SPANISH MOSS TREE AT NOON
(Dedicated to Zora Neale Hurston)

Darlin' water

Can't sink heavy thoughts

Thoughts that dig so deep

They resonate at the Earth's crust

That brimmed hat

Wear it well

Mama

No, it can't shade that glow

Of knowin'

You know

You know

If Eatonville was the

Source of your

Unabashed confidence

In being Black and

In charge

Then let us salute the

Land where Black

Meant power

Your beauty was

Unconventional

Quite marvelous

And although men took
Notice and responded
Honey I know when you said
'I Do'
Your fingers weren't crossed

You had an ink pen behind your
Back
Clicking it when it was time to kiss
Your groom
Because you knew
If your love
For that man ran dry
Somehow your ink
Would always flow…

TELL YOUR PURSE TO MOVE

If you're like me
Then you love a bag
That can dazzle
Razzle
Maybe even waggle

Nothin' like a bag
That will excite
Entice
And make envious women lip bite

But let me tell you
A secret
My great grandmother told me
She rocked me
Propped me
And sat me in a chair
While greasin' her hair

"Baby if you want a purse
One like this…"
With an alligator skin wallet inside
24KT gold inkpen for signing checks
& European lipstick
Accessorized by money lining the folds
"Then listen deep within

To what you are told"

Money is here and gone tomorrow
But that purse
If you take care of it
Will never become bare

It will remain filled
With whatever is
Needed to meet your needs
However never let greed
Replace your needs

Empty that wallet to mothers
And children in need
Don't hold it too close
Let it help and go
Where it's supposed to

Your wallet is yours
Temporarily it serves a
Greater purpose and service
To those who deserve it
Never settle your bag in one place
For too long
Tell your purse to move
And it will lead
You to where you belong

LOVE... I DO

Certain women
Prefer to love
One man
Their entire life

But what about the woman
Who appreciates being loved
by many men?

The strength & courage
Power & enthusiasm
Zeal & fearlessness
Passion & creativity
Spontaneity & compassion
Diligence & gentleness
Love & wisdom
That so uniquely embellishes
Their individual glory

How can their precious love ever
Be quantified
Be compared
Be justified
Enough to make her choose
Just one?

Her love dances off walls

And onto hearts

Into thoughts

That makes her simply unforgettable

Why rob any man of this precious obsession

That is to know her?

Why require each moment surrendered to diary entries

Each gaze unlocked in printed stills

Each laugh released and echoing back no more

Each kiss barrowed only to be added to the leger

Each embrace stolen and now met with demands and requirements

Why limit her right to love freely

And selfishly love herself

More than any of her lovers

More & more exciting

Each time

To know love is amazing

To experience love

In various ways

Is magnificent

Chapter IV: The Truth Hurts

"You delight yourself in the possibility of it all, but fail to see the clear signs of what will never be."

—Woman on the Move's Dilemma

LIVIN' JUST WASN'T WORTH IT

Never mind the speeches,
Saying her beauty is timeless,
She couldn't listen,
She could barely read this.
Her beauty was frozen,
Like she was standing
On the Arctic ocean,
With no motion,
She was hopeless.
He asked her,
Would you like a pastor,
Matter of fact
She wanted a jar of alabaster,
So the perfume would mask her...
Ugliness,
Or so she thought
It was the clothes she bought
The car she drove
And the weaves
That would give her some reprieve
To keep on livin,
Keep on givin,
Until her well ran dry,
Then all her God forsaken ugliness
She could barely hide...
What's so sad was she was so beautiful,

Even her face was musical.

Her eyes although the richest

You'd ever seen,

Were the poorest in vision.

Almost like Self-Hate

Was her True religion.

She hated herself,

So she hated her wealth.

She screamed loudly this aint no life,

"All of that is a lie,

Like an emcee with no mic,

My life is worthless!"

She wanted a man

To give her a reason for livin',

Because life itself wasn't worth it...

-Written in response to 'Consider This' poem "Love" (The Skin You're In)

A FALLEN BLACK QUEEN'S CONTRADICTIONS

What if I call the one

Who caused me to runaway

For guidance?

What if I begged him for food

When he launched the campaign

For my starvation?

What if the one who beat me

Held me like a newborn child

And kept my bruised face close

To his heart?

What if when it was time for

Me to move on to a new love

The only thing I wanted was

For him to tell me who to love?

What if when he left me out in the storm

To fend for myself

He was the only one who would hold up

An umbrella to shelter me?

What if he never saw me

And my last words were

"I hate you, you disgust me!"

But on my deathbed

He knew that

Loving him was the last thought

That entered my mind

THE LAND OF BETTER YET

Honestly I try not to think of you

I'd rather not live in Regret

Or The Land of Better Yet

We made love

In between lines

Better yet

in between rhymes

Because only in our minds

am I your pen

And you're my paper

While coasting on planet: My Time

Our stars couldn't align

When I was with you

Something made me miss you

And then double back

Like why did I miss you

And you forgot me

Like…

How he got free

From my embrace

You let time & space

Take the possibility

Of us away

Like ur my prophecy

& im ur revelation

Why did God not

Move me to your constellation

To love you

And see you

But you're with her

And I'm with him

Yes, I try not to think of you

In that way

Because I'd rather not live in Regret

Or The Land of Better Yet

Now we avoid each other

Like on Bad Poetry's

Motionless elevator

Because you want me to live in Regret

Like every time she's with you

I must regret that I'm not

We might've had a Love Jones

But that's in the Land of Possibility

That I won't dwell in

So I won't live in the Land of Regret

I'll just love

And write

And I might write about you

And what we could do

But that's it

Because she's with you

And I'm with him

And I love him

And you love her

So let's just write poems

About them

And try not to wish

It could have been us

Yes my love,

I try not to think of you

In that way

Because I'd rather not live in Regret

Or The Land of Better Yet

RUNNING ON E

I embrace change

To a certain extent

I resolve to not be

Complacent

In my own eyes

But I have one fatal flaw

I'm scared to move on

From love

I can move on from

A job,

Place,

Friends,

House,

Materialistic things,

But I hate to

Admit when I

Realize my love

Hasn't been reciprocated

Yes, I finally see

My tank has been

Driving

Everyone else

From here to there

But I'm always running myself

On

E.

WOMAN ON THE MOVE'S DILEMMA

When everything in your

Life is changing

And one person

One voice

One familiarity

Throughout all the

Chaos

Is there to comfort

You

Uplift you

And center you

You forget about

The aches and pains

Of leaving

Everything else

Familiar

The lack of a comfort zone

You must go and live

You cling to what's

Barely there

You've held on to it

So long you

Didn't realize when

It let go of you

And when you finally do see

What you've loved for so long

Never loved you back

But was just

There to protect you

From yourself

You focused so much

On what you want

That you act as if

You have already grasped it

You delight yourself

In the possibility

Of it all

But fail to see the clear signs

Of what will never be

So you clung

Until

Finally

He grabbed you by the hand

& visibly let go

So you could finally

See with your own two

Eyes

He was

No longer

There

AWAKENED

One morning I fell asleep

When I should have

Been awoke

My mind had heavy

Thoughts

So many burdens

My brain

Couldn't keep afloat

I dreamt of knights

Without armor &

Horses without knights

I saw darkness

Without stars

And the Sun

Without light

I somehow

Drifted

So deep

My oxygen

Gave way

My body tormented

Twist and turned

Gasping for air

I prayed for

Help

But no one

Was there

Awakened by sunlight

My optimism gave way

I thank God most days

I sleep at night

Chapter V:
Taking No Prisoners

"My body is achin' from chains, flogging, starvation and how fake brothas like you helped them betray u"
– **Why Aren't You Proud to be Black?**

COUNTER-CLOCKWISE

Empty as a dry jar of honey

To a bee

Barren as a tree naked from

A bitter winter breeze

Hopeless as a pirate who

Killed for a ship

With no treasure at sea

Unfulfilled as a man who worked all his life

To only lose all he had in one day

Clocks stop ticking

Because they know

Their time is over

The lion is the most powerful

But the vulture is bolder

Mirrors start cracking when they see me

Because they dare to

Reflect what's on the other side

Eyes won't open because their too

Scared to look

Failure in the eye

BOLD AS YOU LIKE IT!

Call me brazen

If you dare

Maybe trifling

If you so choose

But call me a coward

NEVER!

Call me ostentatious

If you like

Maybe arrogant

If my head is too high

To respond to your antics

But at least I've learned when to follow

Paint me dizzy

If it coats walls

Paint me naïve

If that floats your boat

But don't you dare

Pick up foolish & try it on me!

Paint me stubborn

If my colors won't blend in

Paint me mean

If my cracks become rigid

Since my authenticity threatens you

Then let me paint you a chameleon

The real deal will never cower under pressure

Or blend in when it's time to stand up or speak out!

BIG TALK, LITTLE FEET

Ay baby, say why yo mouth so big

But yo feet so little?

Why can I hear you

Down the street

But up-close

I can barely spot yo feet

Them little feet of yours

Can barely take you to work

But with yo mouth

One would think

You drove to work

Or you didn't cry

When lying alone at night

Or that your lunch bag

Stays empty at mid sunlight

Ay baby, Say why yo mouth so big

But yo feet so little

You sing like a canary

But gets no pay

Your back stay aching

But yo job won't stay

Rebuild yo house

Cuz yo foundation is weak

Close yo mouth

And strap those feet!

TEMPORARY RESOLVE

Maybe I gave you
A part of me too special
Too soon

Maybe I should have
Let you fight
Beg
Plead
And learn my affection

Maybe I should have
Closed my desire
To open your
Mind to new pleasures

Maybe I should have
Stopped the car
Shut the engine off
And released the key
Before the transmission blew

Whatever I should have done
That is clearly
Not what occurred
I haven't earned your trust
Neither have you mine

But don't judge me
I showed you love
The love your mind,
Heart, soul & body longed

I took you to a place
Where you could escape
You could find freedom
And enjoy

I'm sorry if your
Refuge didn't last
As long as you hoped

You came to me
When you should
Have went to God
I know this now
Because you hate me
Because I can't give you
The things that only He can

I'm sorry
I'm human
I gave you all that
I possibly could of
Without betraying myself

Next time do yourself

A favor

And don't run to a woman

For problems that only God

Can solve

Because I can't carry

Your burdens

I was made to love,

Not bare them

BLACKNOGSTIC

Maybe if you stare

Long enough

It will disappear

You see me in the mirror

And walk pass me

Like you don't look like me

What is wrong

With your mind

I'm staring back

At you

Just to remind

You

You are just like me

You pick fights &

Battles with

Men who held you up

When you were

Wounded in war

So you can shake hands

With those who keep you down

Matter of fact

You just recovered

From a public

Beat down

By a racist

Look in the mirror

I do think it's quite

Pitiful that you see my

Blackness

Your Blackness

Staring back at you

Yet you fail

To acknowledge

That I'm here

WHY AREN'T YOU PROUD TO BE BLACK?

Some call it courageous
But why you tryna debate us?
Brotha cut the line
When I dialed 911's operator
Change bonded us
So why you tryna break us?

Some call you 'Haters'
But I call you 'Now & Laters'
You were then a facilitator
For men who believed we were
Savages to separate us
Brotha you don't cry
To embrace us

Your soul longs
For the opportunity to disgrace us
Don't deplete us
To release us
Back in enslavement to beat us
Brotha my ancestors
Paid a heavy price
To release me from these shackles
The way you operate is
Flat out backwards
Explain yourself to us

Why you hate us

Even slavery couldn't break us

It took God to make us

Some other Brotha

Is smarter

Stronger

Shrewder

And

Flat out cooler

So you jealous

I have something

I've been waitin' to tell ya

My body is achin' from chains, floggin', starvation and

How Brothas like you helped them betray us

You betta' learn to respect me

I'm your dispatcher

Keep your eyes straight

Once I help you obtain freedom

Aint no turnin' back

Matter of fact

Let me say it simply

Learn to be proud to be Black!

SUPPORT OR ABORT

The prettiest people

Do the ugliest things

He said 'Support or Abort'

Yep, beautiful and mean

Yes, I like attention

But I don't have time to text, call or argue

When I approached him for guidance

I wanted him to see my view

My intentions were pure

And he had my mind open

So naïve and young

Somethin' brilliant I was hopin'

Experience as a writer

I thought with his expertise

He could take me higher

I never imagined us like a 'we'

Just magical as a pen

And paper can be

I wanted him to direct my vision

To light up the stage

But no he thought I was cute

I supported his curiosity

Aborted our plays

PAUSE

Who wants to take a sabbatical

Play: From love

Maybe a hiatus from

Emotions

Pause:

Complete numbness when

It comes to

Play: Heart pain

Pause:

Maybe a vacation

From late night

Phone calls or texts

Play: Let me turn my back

On your invitations

Pause:

I need rest

Complete mental, emotional

And physical

Deliverance

Play: From your selfish desires

Let me be selfish

Pause:

With my being

Mind

Soul & spirit

Play: As it relates to you

You have emptied

The supply

Pause:

I would feel better

If it quenched your desire

Play: But NO!

The more you take

The more you beg

for me to give

Sorry there's none for me

Pause:

I'm anxiously awaiting

to use these

sick days

AMERICA'S NEW BANDIT (Extended Version)

WARNING:** This poem is not meant for robots, socially impaired, fundamentally indifferent or those who simply don't give a hoot. This poem will cause anger, might send you in a spiral of depression if you are already on edge or if you eat jelly beans all day, brace yourself, this poem may make you feel like some chump just stole some of your last stash of Starburst jelly beans! But anyway, this poem maybe even cause you to question my patriotism, but it is a poem and please read with caution**

Let me label it misguided revenge

Irrevocable racism

With a nice suit

A hint of anything that

Smells like Mr. Buchanan

A Muslim Witch hunt

Instead of the letter A

Let's accidentally label it 'Obama' oops

And pretend like we didn't know

We were comparing our President to a terrorist

To a let's clothe them in turbans

Let's casually call it

'Why does he wear that on his head'

What does the dot mean on her forehead

Why are they here

With a blank stare

And chuckle

Like your existence

Was unequivocally desired

In the land of the free & the brave

He was the 9/11 Mastermind

So he deserves

Death

Matter of Fact, he deserves

To be laid at the guillotine

Yes, let's take it back to 1792

Where men, women & children

Celebrated the death of evil

Criminals by watching them die

As a family

In unison they shout for more blood

Like how some of us

Used to sit and pray

Together as a family

Now the only time

We bond is in death

But what about the American's

Who funded & trained Mujahideen

Notoriously known as the CIA's

Best weapons customers

What terrorist on American

Soil with American blood

Deserves to die

For training al-Qaeda

Why don't we call him

'The Prodigal Son'

In some ways we were like a father

Maybe he was our illegitimate son

But we fathered that terrorist

And now like

Every episode of Maury

We don't want to claim our offspring

Where are those weapons of mass destruction

Did we conveniently never find any

Because that wasn't our sole

Purpose in Afghanistan in the 1st place

What about the estimated

$1 trillion worth of lithium

Discovered in Afghanistan

Before our long overdue exit

They say Avatar is a movie

I think we resemble the criminals

And suck staggering nations dry

So they can come to us

& beg for reprieve

But when they retaliate

They show no mercy

We wonder why we have to

Suffer so gravely

Die so violently

At the blink of an eye

Somebody please tell me

Why they keep calling

The hell whole Osama Bin Laden

Was shuffled through

Like a stack of tattered pinochle cards

A 'mansion'

By what definition is that filth

I wouldn't let a dog

Sleep in

A mansion

Let's over-exaggerate

His life

To make our crimes

Seem less

America's new bandit

Roams freely and without a disguise

There is no need

Our father

Has let us become

What we've become

So we can see

Who the real terrorists are

America's new Bandit

Doesn't wear camouflage

Or carry weapons

America's new bandits

Doesn't hide in caves

They sit alone all day

In houses

Play videogames

And are instructed by

Their mothers to shut up & be quiet

Their fathers ignore them

Better yet

They pretend they don't exist

So these pseudo bastards find solace

In animated versions of life

A life worth living

Of course is better onscreen

Than really lived

They learn to hold in

Their feelings

And discuss their day

To an inanimate object

That can't steer them

Right or wrong

So their just

Left

Alone

With a device

Waiting for the next

Signal to move

The switch

And ignite

A fire in some unsuspecting

Loser

Someone whose life's value is

Supposedly no greater than theirs

Because they don't receive

Hugs, I love you's, or discipline

They just give a

Blank stare

And wait for people

They don't know

To friend them

These are America's New Bandits

In the end

Does it really matter

Who shot first

If you taught me

To shoot

Yes America

We fathered that terrorist

And if we don't wake up,

Change and accept responsibility for our actions

We'll keep breeding more just like him!

Yes, you are still alive

Breathe & Keep Reading

Chapter VI: Sacrificial Love

"It's whispers were so true, so relevant, that I wondered
If this seashell somehow knew me by name"
— **Seashell Whispers**

MY LITTLE CHAMPION

A true fighter
In the sense that he is relentless
On winning his mother's heart
Though the battle has already been won
I let him play the part
My little champion
Is also my hero
Because he saves the day
No matter how tired or
Strict his mother is
For a kiss
He always makes way
Diligent is his pursuit of loving me
Relentless is he at
Always wanting
The title as
Mommy's #1 man
I love my little champion
Indeed I am his biggest fan

CHOCOLATE MOON

Look at you

Chocolate moon

Classy dude

Makes the Sun jealous

He's so cool

The Earth whispers

The ocean opens & closes

Nature consumes

The sky overdoses

Arrogant yet bashful

Diligent & playful

The stars confess that

You are the best

Companion

Aware of your purpose

You ignite the radiance

Of those surrounding you

And you welcome the brilliance

Of others

Who come and go

As more than merely

Passers by

You illuminate

The glory of darkness

Chocolate moon

MY GARDEN'S EMPTY

Gardens are what you make them

I want flowers that

Are always in bloom

So I plant

But every now and then

I forget to water

I just expect them

To grow

And flourish on their own

I pick the prettiest flowers

And plant the strongest seeds

But sometimes

My flowers act as if

I didn't plant them

They forget that I sat next to them

During the warm and cold months

And bared my soul

I laid out in the grass

During the scorching heat

And cried my heart out

To the most beautiful of my garden

Because I hoped they would

Share their brilliance

And give me the love

Back that I gave to them

But my flowers are withering

My garden is barren

The soil isn't fit and I'm left

With only memories

Of my once beautiful garden

I hit it from everyone

So no one knows

The beauty of each

Exotic flower that I once called mine

One day I grew tired

And decided that I no longer

Wanted to fill my water pot

Every flower's need for

Love, care and attention

Finally drained me

And I decided I didn't

Want the responsibility

Of keeping my garden

Now my garden is empty

And it's just me and the Sun.

SEASHELL WHISPERS

My ears listened closely

As my eyes gazed toward the ocean

My heart beat intensely

As this magnificent

Sound revealed the mysteries

Of my being

Hard encased

Sometimes harsh

At first embrace

However its whispers

Were so true

So relevant

That I wondered

If this seashell

Somehow knew me by name

If the ocean had

Tossed it so delicately

Rushed it to and fro

Then at the right moment

Gently whispered my secrets

My wants

Desires

And fears

Had this seashell

Submitted to the ocean

And found me?

WITH LOVE & AT PEACE

As the bell of a wine glass

Sings a melodious hum

With the most delicate touch

So does your hand quiver

At first embrace

If the birds themselves

Would have

Revealed the sensitivity of

A man

To a woman's embrace

I would have

Denied their joyous

Proclamation

I've never experienced something

So beautiful, yet so masculine

As when your lips

Gently kiss my forehead

More surreal is the

Protection I feel

When we walk

With you holding my hand

As you wrap your

Arms around me

And cover me

From the worries

Of everything

Not you and I

The respect and trust

I have for you

Allows me to pray

For your peace and success

In a way

That only a woman

Who loves you

Dearly and deeply

Ever could

SASCHA SKYLAR

Beautiful as the

Western sky

At dusk

My darling

I see my youth

In your eyes

And your grandmother's

Love

In your cheeks

Your skin as bronze

As the fire

In your heart

Your feet as strong

As the determination

Of your mind

Precision like a diamond

Your facets are indeed eternity's greatest

Infinite spectrum

Joyous as a new babe

In her mother's arms

Playful as the

Stars in the sky

A blessing

And a breath of fresh air

STARLIGHT ENCRYPTION

When the moon shines

I gaze at you

Simply amazed at you

For writing my name

On your heart

Though planets and comets

Try to shift us apart

You make way for me

Guide hurtful constellations

Away from me

Just so you can

Make light of the dark

I marvel at you

Because you're so powerful

Yet so beautiful

Even your eyes to me are musical

There's something so magnificent about you

I wonder in what world did we meet

Because before you came into my life

You were already here

Like a faint heartbeat

Surely without you

I wouldn't live

Sometimes I fight your presence

Because I love your presents

But I don't feel worthy of your gifts

Although gifted.i.am

I need someone to choose me to uplift

That's why I think I love you

Because although you know my faults

You sing my praises

Like with you…

Glory ain't neva' pushin' daisies

Because you make way for me

Like you don't push away from me

Or tell me to go

You act as if your love

Will never know life

If I wasn't near you

If my poetry

Couldn't hear you

You make me feel

Like words actually know love

Like if there wasn't a pen and a poem

There would be

No love

Because your words

Light up the stars

Who at night then go and

Add more beats to hearts

And come back to

Light up the sky

Because of you

Baby I believe

Love can fly

79 | Woman on the Move

SOURCES

King, Martin Luther Jr. *The Drum Major Instinct*. 4 February 1968. *Standford, 2011*.
    Web. 09 January 2011.

81 | Woman on the Move

ABOUT THE AUTHOR

Jasira Monique, originally named Monique McDowell was born and raised in West Palm Beach, Florida. She is a writer and entertainer that graduated from Howard University with a B.B.A. in International Business. Her first published book, *Bruised Kisses: Affliction vs. Affection, A Collection of Poems* was released in April 2009 by Publish America. *Bruised Kisses* has been featured on local news and radio shows such as WXEL South Florida Artsview, Channel 9 News in Denver and various online publications. Jasira Monique is an active volunteer and advocate for youth and has launched the *iLive Campaign*, www.iLiveCampaign.org. As Ms. Florida Plus America 2012, Monique promotes mental health awareness and suicide prevention. A portion of proceeds from *Woman on the Move* will help mental health organizations and affected families in need. To learn more about Jasira Monique's work or how you can support please visit www.jasiramonique.com

www.ingramcontent.com/pod-product-compliance
Lightning Source LLC
Chambersburg PA
CBHW031205090426
42736CB00009B/785